# Contents

Any words appearing in bold, **like this**, are explained in the Glossary.

About the experiments and demonstrations

In this book you will find sections called 'Science Answers'. These describe an activity that you can try yourself. Here are some safety rules to follow:

- Ask and adult to help with any cutting using a sharp knife.
- Mains electricity is dangerous. Never, ever try to experiment with it.

Materials you will use

Most of the activities can be carried out with objects that you can find in your own home. But a few will need items that you can buy from a hardware shop.

 **WARNING**

Never look at the Sun, or at any very bright light, either directly or through a telescope or binoculars – this could permanently damage your eyesight.

What is light?

We live in a world flooded with **light**. Even before the Sun rises, its light makes the sky bright, lighting up the Earth. When the sky is covered with thick clouds, the day is gloomy, but a lot of the Sun's light still comes through the clouds. At night, and on dull days, we use light made by human beings. Electric light bulbs and **fluorescent lamps** light up homes and offices. Outside, street lights shine out to show us our way.

Light is all around us, but we cannot hear it or feel it. We become aware of it when it enters our eyes. Whenever we see an object, it is because light has travelled from that object into our **eyes**. Light is what makes it possible for us to see.

Where does light come from?

Some objects make the light (or most of the light) that they send out. We say that they emit or 'give out' light. Examples are the Sun and stars; light bulbs, when they are turned on; fires and fireflies. We call these objects light-sources. But most objects are not light-sources. They send light to our eyes after first receiving it from other objects that do give out light. This is called **reflecting** light. The Moon, for example, does not give out light of its own. We see it because it reflects light from the Sun. After the Sun has set, the Moon still reflects its light to us.

How far can light travel?

Light from the Sun travels 150 million kilometres to reach the Earth. It takes eight minutes to do so. But light from the farthest galaxies (star-systems) that we can see with the naked eye has travelled for trillions upon trillions of kilometres, and taken over two million years. And large **telescopes** can detect very faint galaxies thousands of times farther away than these.

SCIENCE ANSWERS

Light

FROM SUN TO BULBS

Heinemann

www.heinemann.co.uk/library

Visit our website to find out more information about **Heinemann Library** books.

To order:

☎ Phone 44 (0) 1865 888066

🖷 Send a fax to 44 (0) 1865 314091

💻 Visit the Heinemann Bookshop at www.heinemann.co.uk/library to browse our catalogue and order online.

Editorial: Sarah Eason and Georga Godwin
Design: Jo Hinton-Malivoire and
  Tinstar Design Ltd (www.tinstar.co.uk)
Illustrations: Jeff Edwards
Picture Research: Rosie Garai
  and Liz Eddison
Production: Viv Hichens

Originated by Ambassador Litho Ltd
Printed and bound in China by WKT

ISBN 0 431 17494 6 (hardback)
07 06 05 04 03
10 9 8 7 6 5 4 3 2 1

ISBN 0 431 17502 0 (paperback)
08 07 06 05 04
10 9 8 7 6 5 4 3 2 1

British Library Cataloguing in Publication Data

Cooper, Christopher
Light. – (Science Answers)
535
A full catalogue record for this book is available from the British Library.

Acknowledgements

The Publishers would like to thank the following for permission to reproduce photographs: Corbis/Bettman **pp. 28, 28a**; Corbis/Jeremy Horner **p. 13**; Corbis/Lawrence Manning **p. 10**; Corbis/Robert Holmes **p. 18**; Corbis/Roger Ressmeyer **p. 29**; Liz Eddison **pp. 16, 17**; Photodisc **pp. 5, 20, 22**; Science Photo Library/Adam Hart-Davis **p. 9**; Science Photo Library/Damien Lovegrove **p. 12**; Science Photo Library/John Durham **p. 24**; Taxi/Getty Images/Don Herbert **p. 26**; Taxi/Getty Images/Ron Chapple **p. 27**; Taxi/Getty Images/Willie Maldonado **p. 21**; Trevor Clifford **pp. 15, 23**; Tudor Photography **pp. 6, 11, 14**.

Cover photograph of the aurora borealis reproduced with permission of Science Photo Library/Chris Madeley.

The Publishers would like to thank Robert Snedden and Barbara Katz for their assistance with the preparation of this book.

Every effort has been made to contact copyright holders of any material reproduced in this book. Any omissions will be rectified in subsequent printings if notice is given to the Publishers.

City lights

Modern cities blaze with light at night. Lighting in homes and workplaces runs on electricity that comes from power stations.

How do we make light?

Nowadays most of the **light** we make ourselves comes from electric light bulbs. But human beings were once dependent on candles made of animal fats and oil **lamps** burning vegetable oils. It was not until the end of the 19th century that both gas and electricity were used for lighting in the home.

How does a switch make the light come on?

Nowadays the **incandescent** (hot and glowing) light bulb is the major form of lighting almost everywhere. Light bulbs contain a length of coiled wire, called a **filament**, made of the metal tungsten. Electric current flows through this when you flip the switch. The current makes the tungsten hot and so it glows. Large bulbs using strong electric current are used in lighting large spaces in hotels and offices. Small bulbs using the weak current from a battery are used in pocket torches.

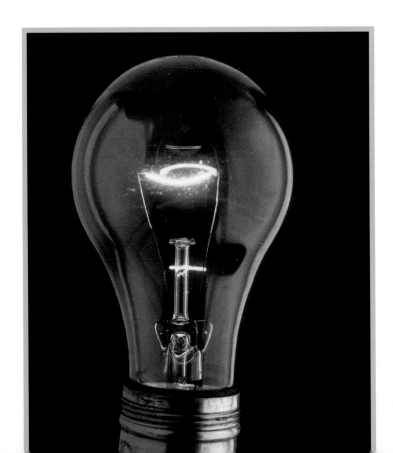

EXPERIMENT: What makes a light bulb brighter?

HYPOTHESIS:
Increasing the current through a bulb increases its brightness.

EQUIPMENT:
A torch bulb, two flat batteries (the type usually used in cycle-lamps, with flexible metal contacts), three lengths of electric flex (plastic-coated electric wire), each about 20 cm long.

EXPERIMENT STEPS:
1 Scrape off about 3 cm of the plastic coating from each end of each piece of flex to show the metal wire inside.
2 Twist the metal end of one piece of flex around a contact on one of the batteries.
3 Twist the end of another piece around the other contact on the battery.
4 Touch the two free ends to the contacts on the bulb. Note how brightly the bulb shines.
5 Connect both batteries, as shown. You must attach the positive (+) terminal of one to the negative (–) terminal of the other.
6 Now touch the free ends of the wires to the bulb again.
7 Note whether the bulb is brighter with one battery or two.
8 Write down what you saw.

flex

bulb

battery

CONCLUSION:
A bigger current produces a brighter light.

How do we see things?

We often see beams of sunlight passing through a hole in a curtain or window blind, or through gaps in clouds. A very thin beam is called a ray of light. We can see an object when light rays are reflected from the object into our **eyes**.

Waves of light

Light is made up of **waves**. There are many sorts of wave around us. There are waves in water and sound waves in the air. Light waves are different from other sorts of wave in an important way. As a water wave spreads outwards the water moves up and down at each place. This is shown by a cork, which will bob up and down as the wave passes it. But in a light wave, nothing moves in this way. Light can travel even in completely empty space, where there isn't even any air, so there is nothing that can move.

But in a light wave, though there is nothing moving, there is something that is changing all the time. A light wave has electrical and magnetic effects wherever it passes. For example, a light wave can make an electric current flow when it strikes a **photoelectric cell** on a **solar-powered** calculator, so making the calculator work. Scientists say the light wave consists of an **electromagnetic field**. The field changes in strength and direction all the time.

What happens inside the eye?

Light rays first pass through the clear front of the eyeball, or **cornea**. Behind the cornea is the coloured part of the eye, called the **iris**. The light rays pass through the **pupil**, a hole in the iris and then through the eye's **lens**, a piece of **transparent** tissue. After travelling through clear liquid inside the eye the rays finally strike the **retina**, the inside back surface of the eyeball.

The lens acts like the lens in a camera. It alters the direction of the light rays to form an upside-down **image**, or picture, on the retina. Thousands of nerves send **signals** (tiny electric currents) from the retina to the brain. The signals carry information about the **colour** and brightness of the light at each point in the image.

Can we see in the dark?

We cannot see when it is completely dark – that is, when there is no light at all. But the eye can improve its ability to see when there is a little light. The pupil, or window, at the front can grow larger in order to let in as much light as possible.

When the light gets too bright, the pupil grows smaller to shut out some of the light. You can see the difference in a friend's pupils or your own, if you use a mirror. Look at the pupils indoors in faint light and then outside in sunshine.

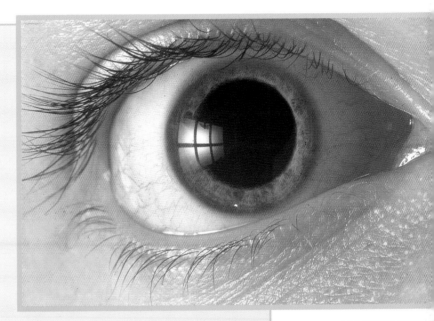

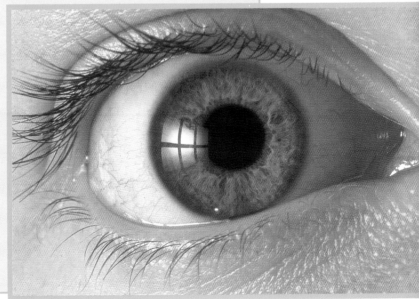

How can we tell how far away things are?

The brain has several ways of working out how far away something is. The size of its image on the retina is important: the farther away something is, the smaller the image.

Also, the images on both retinas are slightly different. Objects appear at slightly different places in each image. When we look at a nearby object, we turn our eyes inwards slightly so that both of them are looking directly at it. The two images of the object are then at the same positions on the two retinas. The brain can judge the object's distance from the amount by which the eyes turn in.

Defending against dazzle

We can often be dazzled by sunlight that is too bright. Sunglasses block some of the light from passing through. Because less light reaches the eyes of the wearer, the scene looks less bright, though bright enough for most activities.

EXPERIMENT: How does the eye bend light rays?

HYPOTHESIS:

Rounded, transparent objects (like eyeballs and eye lenses) alter light rays and form images.

EQUIPMENT:

A drinking glass with straight sides, filled with water.

EXPERIMENT STEPS:

1 Pour water into the glass and hold objects up behind the glass. Use pictures, printed words, patterns, your own hand.
2 Write down how this affects the appearance of the objects.
3 Alter the distance between the glass and the objects behind, and write down the result.
4 Do the same things with glasses of other sizes, if you have any.

CONCLUSION:

You should have noticed that the water in the glass strongly affected the way things behind it looked. It made things that were close look larger. Objects farther away looked as if they'd been flipped from left to right. At the edges of the glass the objects looked so strongly altered in shape that they were hard to recognize. Those changes were the result of light rays bending as they passed through the water-filled glass.

The eyeball is also curved, although it is shaped like a globe, not a cylinder as the glass is. The eye-lens has a curved shape, too. The eye-lens and the front part of the eye bend light rays entering the eye. Unlike the glass, they have just the right shape and size to form an image on the retina.

How does light move?

Misleading mirrors

When a light ray falls on a mirror, the reflected ray makes the same angle with the surface that the first ray made. Just as the original light rays spread out from the object, the reflected rays spread out as if coming from a place behind the mirror. However, because the rays have been reflected, they appear the opposite way round in a mirror. This is called a mirror **image**.

When you cross a street, you rely on cars being in the direction they seem to be. You assume they are in the direction from which the **light** has come, because light travels in straight lines. And that is true most of the time. But sometimes the direction of light rays is altered, and then things seem to be in the wrong places. That is what mirrors do.

Most objects have rough surfaces that reflect light waves in all directions. Mirrors have very smooth surfaces, which reflect the light in a special way. It looks as if there is an object behind the mirror. We often call this a 'reflection' of the object, but the proper name is 'image'.

A mirror made of air

In the desert, a layer of hot air near the ground can act like a mirror. It **reflects** the sky, just as a lake of water would. This has often misled travellers.
The image is called a **mirage**.

What's funny in the Hall of Mirrors?

A distorting mirror at a funfair has a 'wavy' surface. The top part of the mirror may form an image of your head that is wider than normal, while the part just below may form an image of your chest that seems even fatter. So in the mirror your head and neck seem to be stretched out. This is because the light that hits the mirror at different places is reflected from the surface in different directions.

How fast does light travel?

When you switch on a light, it only takes a hundred-millionth of a second for light to flood the room. This is because light travels at a fantastic **speed**, almost 300,000 kilometres per second.

Can light bend?

Light travels more slowly in **transparent** materials, such as glass, water or air, than it does in completely empty space. In water its speed is 3/4 of its empty-space speed. In glass it is about 2/3 of that speed. In air the speed of light is reduced by less than a thousandth of its empty-space speed.

Light rays bend whenever they change speed. For example, light bends when it passes from air into water and is slowed down. This bending causes a straw or a spoon to look bent when it is dipped in a transparent liquid like a glass of water.

EXPERIMENT: What effects do differently shaped mirrors have on images?

HYPOTHESIS:

Differently curved surfaces will distort images in different ways.

EQUIPMENT:

A large, shiny spoon (a soup ladle is even better), an ordinary flat mirror.

EXPERIMENT STEPS:

1 Hold the spoon in front of you. Look into the outside of the bowl of the spoon. This is the **convex** side. Move the ladle or spoon closer to your **eye** and then farther away. Notice what happens to the image. Compare what you see in the flat mirror.

2 Now look into the inside of the bowl of the spoon, the **concave** side. Again move the ladle or spoon closer to your eye and then farther away.

3 Write down what you saw.

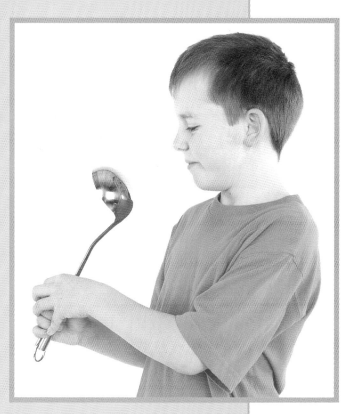

CONCLUSION:

A convex mirror gives an image that is the right way up but smaller than the one made by a flat mirror.

A concave mirror produces a **magnified** image of you when you are very close. When you are far away, the image is upside-down and smaller than the one made by an ordinary mirror.

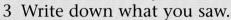

What are shadows?

A **shadow** is not a real object. It is just a place – on the ground or a wall or some other surface – that is receiving less **light** than the area around it. It is receiving less light because something is blocking out some of the light that other nearby areas are getting. Light cannot get into the shadow area because to do so it would have to bend. Light generally travels in straight lines.

For example, when you stand out of doors in the sunlight, light cannot pass through your body. Some is **reflected**, and some is **absorbed**, or taken in, by your body. There is an area on the ground that this light does not reach, and this is your shadow.

Why are shadows not completely dark?

You can still see things on the ground where your shadow is. This is because some light is able to get to that place. The light comes from the sky, or is reflected from surrounding buildings and other objects.

Does everything block light?

All materials block some light, but the amount varies. Some materials let through a lot of light but make things look fuzzy and blurred. Such materials are called **translucent**. An example is 'frosted' glass, which has a rough surface, and is used for bathroom windows. Other examples are flimsy materials such as muslin.

A material that completely blocks light is called **opaque**. An object or material that lets through most of the light, such as a window, is called **transparent**. Air and clear water are also transparent. But even the most transparent materials absorb and reflect a little of the light. If a ray of light passes through several pieces of glass, each piece of glass absorbs a little more of the light. Things seen through them are darkened compared with things seen through one piece of glass.

Why are shadows different lengths?

Shadows are different depending on where the light source is that is creating the shadow. You can see the effect by holding a desk **lamp** in the air and moving it about above objects on the desktop. Some shadows will be shorter than the objects; others will be longer, depending on where the lamp is shining. The Sun has the same effect. When the Sun is high in the sky, shadows are short. When the Sun is lower in the sky, shadows are long.

Time telling from the Sun

Sundials were once widely used to tell the time. This modern sundial is a fun feature in a park.

EXPERIMENT: How good a timekeeper is the Sun?

HYPOTHESIS:
A sundial can show how 'fast' or 'slow' the Sun is compared with the true time.

EQUIPMENT:
A stick at least 60 cm long, ten ping-pong balls or white-painted pebbles, or other markers, a watch, clock or portable radio (for time signals), a waterproof marker.

EXPERIMENT STEPS:
1 Set the stick upright in the soil in an unused part of your garden.
2 Draw part of a circle about 1 metre from the stick on its northern side (on the southern side if you live south of the equator).
3 On a sunny day, on each hour mark the point on the circle that the stick's shadow is pointing towards (if the shadow is short) or where the shadow crosses it (if the shadow is long).
4 Press a marker into the ground at this point and label it with the hour (10 a.m., 11 a.m., etc.).
5 On each sunny day after that, compare the time shown by the sundial with the correct time. Draw a table showing how much the Sun is ahead of or behind the true time through the year.

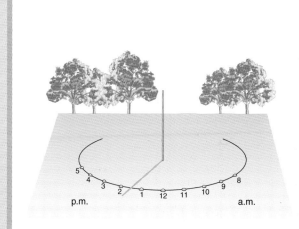

CONCLUSION:
This simple sundial is accurate at some times of the year, but more than an hour wrong at others. The Sun itself can be up to about 15 minutes fast or slow at different times of year! (This is because of the varying speed of the Earth in its orbit around the Sun.)

Why do things look coloured?

The **colours** we see depend on the **light** that enters our **eyes**. If the light entering your eye from the cover of a book lying on the table is red (or mostly red) and if your eye is working normally, then the book looks red.

Sunlight is a mixture of light waves of many different colours. This mixture looks white to the human eye. If an object **reflects** all these colours, then when the reflected light enters a human eye, the object looks white. But the red book **absorbs**, or takes in, some of the colours of light and reflects (sends back) the red light. That is why it looks red.

If another book next to the red book reflects mainly green light and absorbs other colours, then it looks green.

Bright and beautiful

National flags use bright, rich colours so that they stand out and attract the attention of the onlooker. We could not see any of these colours if they weren't already present in the sunlight falling on the flags.

Why do things look different in coloured light?

You can alter the colour that something looks by altering the colour of the light shining on it. If you put a red bulb into a **lamp**, the appearance of the things in the room will be altered. The green book will not be able to reflect any green light, because there is (almost) no green light in the light from the red bulb. So the green book will reflect very little light and will look dark. But the red book will reflect the red light from the bulb and will look much as it looks in ordinary light. The white paper will also reflect the red light and will look red. If a green bulb is used, the green book and the paper will both look green. The red book will now be the one that looks dark.

Can colours be separated?

Sunlight is white light. The colours mixed up in sunlight often become separated. Light is **refracted** as it enters glass, water or a gemstone. Violet rays are refracted the most, red rays the least, and other colours by in-between amounts. If the material is angled like the faces of a gemstone, or curved like a water droplet, the colours are separated even more when the light comes out of the material.

When this separated light shines on a wall or other surface, it forms a band of multicoloured light, called a **spectrum**. A **rainbow** is a spectrum, too. Rainbows are formed when sunlight is refracted and broken up into different colours when it passes through raindrops.

EXPERIMENT: How can we find out what colours of light are reflected by an object?

HYPOTHESIS:

Transparent coloured materials show us each colour in the reflected light separately.

EQUIPMENT:

Some 'colour filters' (materials that let through only some colours – try transparent coloured sweet wrappings, coloured gift wrap or pieces of coloured plastic).

EXPERIMENT STEPS:

1 Place a few coloured objects, pictures and so on together in a bright light. They can be differently coloured sweets or buttons, or anything that is colourful and interesting.
2 View the objects through each of your filters in turn.
3 Make a table with columns headed 'Object', 'Filter colour' and 'Brightness'.
4 In the table, write 'bright', 'medium' or 'dark' to show how bright each object looks through each filter.

CONCLUSION:

Suppose you find that a blue object looks bright through a blue filter. That means that the object reflects mainly blue light. If it looks dark through a red filter, then it reflects only a little red light.

You might find that it looks medium bright through a green filter. This explains why the object looks blue – blue light is the main part of the mixture of colours in the light that it sends to your eye.

How do lenses help us see?

Cameras, **microscopes**, **telescopes**, eyeglasses, even the human **eye** itself, all use **lenses** to make **images**. Lenses are pieces of **transparent** material shaped to bend light rays in special ways. A **magnifying** glass is a single lens. Eyeglasses consist of two lenses held in a frame.

How do lenses work?

If you have glasses, or if you can borrow a pair, you can see how they affect the way things look while you hold them in your hands (rather than wearing them). Some lenses act like magnifying glasses. Others are differently shaped and make things look smaller.

How can we see the very small?

Microscopes let us see objects that are far too small to see with our unaided eyes. Microscopes consist of many lenses, very accurately shaped and positioned. They bend the light rays coming from a small object underneath the microscope so that to the person looking through the microscope they seem to be coming from a large object. This picture shows tiny plant cells seen through a microscope.

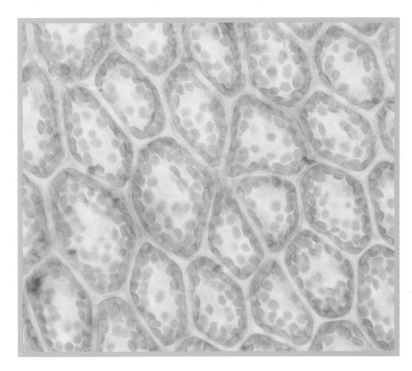

EXPERIMENT: How can we make a magnifying glass stronger?

HYPOTHESIS:
Two magnifying glasses are stronger than one.

EQUIPMENT:
Two inexpensive magnifying glasses from a toyshop.

EXPERIMENT STEPS:
1 Look at some nearby objects with one of the magnifying glasses. Notice how much the objects seem increased in size.
2 Notice the effect of holding the lens far from an object. It produces an upside-down image that appears to be between you and the lens.
3 Examine this image using the second magnifying glass. According to where you hold the second lens, you can form a final image that is either the right way up or upside-down, and bigger than the first image.

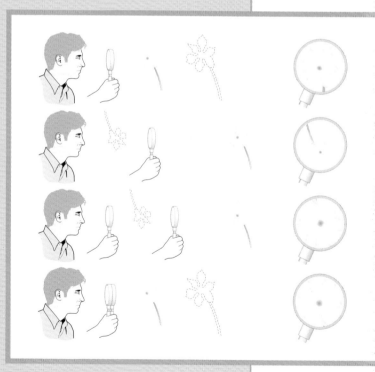

4 Now hold the two lenses together as if they were one lens and see how much they magnify.

5 Write down what you saw.

CONCLUSION:
Two lenses can be more powerful than either one by itself, depending on how they are positioned in relation to each other.

Is there light we cannot see?

Scientists were amazed when they discovered, about 200 years ago, that **invisible light** exists. In fact, most of the light that comes from the Sun and from **lamps** is invisible.

What's beyond the spectrum we can see?

When your skin gets tanned, it's an invisible part of the sunlight that's doing it. This light is called **ultraviolet** (UV) light. 'Ultraviolet' means 'beyond violet'. UV light is called this because, when sunlight is spread out into a **spectrum**, the invisible ultraviolet rays occur just outside the visible spectrum, next to the visible violet rays. The ultraviolet light can be detected because it affects photographic film and electronic instruments – as well as tanning skin.

We cannot see ultraviolet light, but many other creatures, such as birds and bees, can.

Dangers of UV

When UV light in sunlight falls on your skin, it passes into the skin and triggers chemical reactions. Body cells in the skin make a dark substance called melanin, which blocks the UV and protects the body. Exposure to too much UV for a long time is dangerous and can cause skin disease later in life. The risk is reduced if people avoid tanning, by staying in the shade and keeping covered in the middle of the day, when sunlight is brightest. Sun creams help a little, by blocking out some of the UV.

Heat radiation

Beyond the red light at the other end of the spectrum is invisible infrared (IR) light – more usually called **infrared radiation**. ('Infrared' means 'below red'.) You can feel IR radiation as warmth on your skin. Infrared rays come from all the objects around us, including our own bodies. The warmer an object is, the more IR radiation it sends out. It is possible to take photographs and make **television** (TV) pictures using the infrared radiation from a scene. Remote control units control TV sets and other electronic equipment with pulses of infrared radiation.

People who found the answers

Thomas Young (1773–1829)

The English doctor and scientist, Thomas Young, was a brilliant student at school, who mastered many languages. He became interested in **light** when learning how the **eye** works when he was studying to become a doctor. He showed that muscles in the eye change the shape of the **lens** in order to focus on objects.

Young suggested that we have three sorts of light-sensitive detector in the eye, each triggered most strongly by particular **colours** of light. The different strengths of the **signals** that they send to the brain produce all the different colour sensations that we have. Young also did experiments in which he showed that light consists of **waves**.

Jean-Bernard-Léon Foucault (1819–1868)

Foucault worked on the problem of the **speed** of light, bouncing a beam of light off a rotating mirror. The light travelled to a fixed mirror a few metres away and was **reflected** back along its own path. But when the mirror was spinning extremely fast, it moved through a tiny angle in the time between the moment when the light was reflected from the revolving mirror and the moment that it returned. So the light was reflected at a slight angle. By measuring this angle, Foucault was able to work out the speed of light. He arrived at the value of 298,000 kilometres per second, very close to the correct figure of 299,792 kilometres per second.

Amazing facts

- **Light waves** have an extremely short **wavelength**. Red **light** has the longest wavelength, but even this is less than a thousandth of a millimetre. Violet light has the shortest wavelength, which is about half of the wavelength of red light, or one-third of a thousandth of a millimetre.

- The distance to the Moon has been measured by bouncing light from it. The astronauts who visited the Moon between 1969 and 1972 left mirrors there, pointing towards the Earth. Later, flashes of light from powerful **lasers** were fired from the Earth. The **reflected** light took about 2.5 seconds to travel the approximately 384,000 kilometres (239,000 miles) to the Moon and then back again. Scientists measured the time very accurately and so found the distance to within a few centimetres.

- Some animals can feel **infrared radiation** far more accurately than we can. Some types of snake, including pit vipers, rattlesnakes and pythons, have infrared-detecting organs in their heads. The snakes can detect the warmth from their prey, such as mice, when it is too dark to see anything by visible light.

- You can sometimes see the **shadow** of the Earth. The Moon sometimes enters the Earth's shadow. It is then partly or wholly darkened, because the Moon shines only by reflecting the light of the Sun. This is called an eclipse of the Moon. In some years there are no eclipses of the Moon; in others there can be one, two or even three.

Glossary

absorb take in, swallow up – most objects absorb some light, while the rest of the light bounces back or passes through

colour sensation produced by the eye and brain when light enters the eye. Colour depends on the various wavelengths in the light.

concave curved like the inside of a bowl, with the centre farther away from the viewer than the outside

convex curved like the outside of a bowl, with the centre closer to the viewer than the outside

cornea clear front part of the eyeball

electromagnetic field pattern of electrical and magnetic influences. An electromagnetic field can make electric currents flow, or affect magnets. Light waves consist of fast-changing electromagnetic fields.

eye organ in human beings and many other animals that detects light

filament in an electric light-bulb, a hot glowing metal wire

fluorescent lamp lamp consisting of a hollow tube filled with gas at low pressure. When an electric current passes through the gas, the gas gives out invisible ultraviolet light. A special material coating the inside of the tube absorbs the ultraviolet light and fluoresces, giving out visible light.

image picture of something

incandescent hot and glowing

infrared radiation waves that are like visible light, but with wavelengths too long to be seen by the human eye

invisible not able to be seen

iris coloured part of the eye that controls how much light is let in

lamp device containing something that produces light, such as burning oil or gas, or a glowing metal wire

laser device that produces a beam of light that is of one very precise wavelength

lens piece of transparent material shaped to bend the path of light rays so that they form an image

light 1) waves to which our eyes are sensitive, enabling us to see the surrounding world 2) also applied to ultraviolet and infrared waves

magnify/magnifying make something look bigger

microscope instrument containing lenses arranged to magnify small objects

mirage misleading appearance of something in the distance caused when light rays are bent as they travel through layers of air of different temperatures

opaque not letting light through

photoelectric cell device that generates electricity when light strikes it

pupil hole in the iris at the front of the eye, through which light enters the eye

rainbow curved band of glowing colours formed in the sky when sunlight is reflected and refracted by raindrops

reflect/reflection bouncing back of light when it strikes a surface

refraction bending of light when it travels from one material into another

retina layer at the back of the eye that is sensitive to light

shadow place that receives less light than nearby places because some light is blocked out by an opaque object

speed how fast something moves. Light speed is measured in metres per second.

signal in nerves, signals are electric currents that carry information to the brain about what is happening in the body

solar power power produced from sunlight

spectrum 1) band of colour produced when a beam of light is spread out so that the different wavelengths in it are separated 2) range of different wavelengths produced when any waves – light, infrared, ultraviolet or others – are spread out according to their wavelengths

telescope instrument containing lenses or mirrors arranged to form a magnified image of a distant object

television device for producing a moving image of what is happening at another place

translucent describes a material that you can see through, but not clearly, like muslin

transparent describes a material that you can see through clearly, like ordinary window glass

ultraviolet light waves that are like visible light, but with wavelengths too short to be seen by the human eye

wave 1) wave in matter consists of vibrating particles – each particle moves back and forth in one place while the vibration spreads through the material 2) light wave consists of an electromagnetic field varying rapidly at each point, while the wave as a whole moves forward

wavelength distance from one crest of a wave to the next

Index

More books to read

Science Fact Files: Light and Sound, Steve Parker
   (Hodder Wayland, January, 2001)
Hands on Science: Rainbows to Lasers: Projects with Light,
   Kathryn Whyman (Franklin Watts, 1989)
Flying Start Science: Light, Kim Taylor (Belitha Press, 1994)
Exploring Science: Exploring Light, Ed Catherall
   (Hodder Wayland, 1989)